David E. Nye

Introducing Denmark and the Danes
— a two hour briefing

Introducing Denmark and the Danes
© David E. Nye and University Press of Southern Denmark
Layout, set and printed by Narayana Press
Cover design by Anne Charlotte Mouret, UniSats

Revised 5th edition, 2nd impression 2012
ISBN: 978-87-7674-128-0

Photographs in the book:

Polfoto (pages 7, 15, 27, 29, 31, 45, 51, 59, 67)
Scanpix (pages 39, 63)

Map page 6 © Birger Bromann
Drawings pages 9, 36 and 43 © Bjerne Johansen
Photograph page 12 © Sund & Bælt
Photograph page 31 by kind permission of Her Majesty the Queen of Denmark and Bjørn Nørgaard
Photograph page 35 © Steen Larsen
Photograph page 41 © Morten Marboe
Photograph page 53 © Vestas Wind Systems A/S
Photograph pages 69 and 71 © The Copenhagen Post

Cover:
Polfoto

Mechanical, photographic or other reproduction
of this book or portions of it is not permitted
under Danish copyright laws.

University Press of Southern Denmark
Campusvej 55
5230 Odense M.
Denmark

www.universitypress.dk

Table of Contents

Preface *5*

1. Cultural Background *7*
Stereotypes *7*
Geography and Population *10*
Immigration *16*
Class Structure *18*
The Family *20*
Language *22*
Cultural Influence from Abroad *24*

2. National Character *29*
Egalitarians? *29*
Leadership *32*
The Daily Round *34*
Housing *37*
Socializing *38*
Meals *40*
Evenings Out *42*
Alcohol *44*
Smoking *45*
The Educational System *46*

3. Economics and Politics *51*
Trade and the Economy *51*
Energy *54*
Employment *56*
Taxes *56*
The Welfare State *57*
Politics *59*
Foreign Affairs *62*

4. Practical Advice for Visitors 69

Get Registered 69
Travel inside Denmark 70
Working in Denmark 72
Finding Accommodation 72
What to bring? What to buy? 73
The Danish Climate 73
Holidays in Denmark 74
Learning Danish 75
Libraries and Books 76
Danish National Newspapers 77
Last words 78
Denmark's University Webpages 79
Calling Denmark from abroad 79

Preface

This little book began as one in a series of short works designed by FUHU (the Danish Society for the Advancement of Business Education) to introduce students to nations that they would visit in the course of their studies.

The rest of the series was written by Danes with long experience living abroad, but as a foreigner long resident in Denmark, I was asked to write the volume on Denmark, which first appeared in 1991 and has sold briskly ever since.

This considerably expanded and completely updated edition is for anyone who wants to get oriented to Denmark. It points out things that are so obvious to the Danes themselves that they might not think it necessary to explain them.

It is not a conventional guidebook, but falls somewhere between scholarship, journalism, and personal opinion. It is scholarly in the sense that all names, dates, and statistics are as accurate as possible. It is journalistic in that the writing is uncomplicated and generalizes about a large subject in a small space.

It can only be a curiosity to Danes, but it introduces outsiders to a remarkable country and helps them to find their way into its culture.

Cultural Background

Stereotypes

In 1988 a 12 year-old Danish girl went to the United States with her parents for a year and attended the local school. Early in the first term, the teacher asked her to show the class where she came from, using a map in the history book. She turned to a map of Europe, but much to her shock, Denmark was not there. Some of the islands were vaguely sketched in, but a reader could not tell if they were part of Sweden or Germany. She was too amazed to be embarrassed, and pointed out the book's error with some emphasis. She had just learned that Danes abroad often must contend not so much with stereotypes as with ignorance.

Most people at least know where France, Japan, China, or Germany are on a map, and most people have a few ideas about what these nations are like. Denmark is far less known, and many have somewhat diffuse ideas about it, like an island only glimpsed through the mist and fog. Some assume that Scandinavians are much alike, mixing together Swedes, Norwegians, and Danes in a hazy vision of blond people living in a snow-bound welfare state in northern Europe.

For those who know it, however, Denmark is quite distinct from its Scandinavian neighbors. It has a long history, and at least until c. 1630 it was one of the great European powers. Yet, today it is a small country, and visitors may perhaps be forgiven for knowing little about it on arrival. Some people have ideas about it that, like the American textbook, are entirely incorrect. Presumably you know that Copenhagen is not the capital of Sweden and that the language of Denmark is neither Dutch nor Denmarkese. You may rightly suspect that most of that famous pornography is sold to tourists, and you probably know that Danes are seldom brooding Hamlets who act as if they were suffering an existential crisis in an Ingmar Bergman film. (Besides, Bergman is Swedish.) But can you sort out true from false in the following statements?

- The best time to visit is July, when one can enjoy the midnight sun.
- Like Norway, Denmark often wins gold medals at the winter Olympics.
- Denmark is a predominantly agricultural country.
- Its chief exports are bacon, cheese, butter, and other foodstuffs.
- Like the other Nordic countries, Denmark's hilly terrain and cold winters make it ideal for skiers and skaters.
- Denmark is a welfare state that controls virtually all services, such as the telephone company.

All of these statements are false. Denmark is mostly flat, and the highest point is only 568 feet above the sea. The second highest elevation is but 482 feet high, even if the

Danes call it Heaven Mountain (*Himmelbjerget*). Obviously, compared to most nations, Denmark has only hills, and cannot build a proper downhill ski resort. The country does not even send a team to the winter Olympics, although individuals do participate, some coming from Greenland. Furthermore, Denmark is too far south to enjoy the midnight sun or to get certain, regular snowfall.

The major winter sports other than European football are played indoors: handball and badminton. The temperate climate does make it an ideal agricultural nation, justly famous for bacon, cheese, and milk products, and two-thirds of the land is used for farming. For seventy years, however, the country has been predominantly industrial, and industrial goods and services make up the lion's share of exports. Denmark has a mixed economy, with few state-run businesses. The telephone service is private, with several competing companies, and although most other services are public, they are not always free. If you failed parts of this informal test, read on.

Not much snow in Denmark.

Geography and Population

Most people think of Denmark as a small country on Germany's northern border, not realizing that the Kingdom of Denmark also contains Greenland and the Faroe Islands (north of Britain's Shetland Islands). Both are subject to the Danish sovereign, but neither is a member of the European Union. Denmark was a major force in European affairs until the Napoleonic Wars. Present-day Norway was long part of Denmark, as was the southern part of present-day Sweden.

As recently as 1864 the country included part of Northern Germany. Iceland belonged to Denmark until World War II. Greenland (only 55,000 people but 840,000 square miles) and the Faroe Islands (44,000 people and an estimated 3.5 million birds) are the last remnants of the empire. Both now have forms of self-rule and they talk of full independence, although both would like to keep getting Danish economic subsidies. Neither will be discussed further here, as they have separate political systems and distinctive cultures, but these resource-rich areas will likely remain a part of Denmark's future, as well as a reminder of its past.

European Denmark may be small, but because it is broken up into one peninsula and many islands, it takes considerable time to visit all parts of it. Many tourists only get to know Copenhagen and its island of Sjælland (spelled Zealand on English maps). When sailing vessels were the world's only transport system, this location was hardly a handicap, and today its position in the Baltic Sea remains a great advantage, making Copenhagen a key commercial center for the region.

Indeed, the expansion of the European Union to include Sweden, Finland, Poland and the Baltic States increases this centrality. Within Denmark, the islands of Lolland and Falster to the south are poorer regions that increasingly have come within Copenhagen's orbit; together these three islands contain about half of Denmark's 5.4 million inhabitants. The other half live west of the wide channel between Zealand and Funen, called the *Storebælt* (the Great Belt).

Danes once perceived this channel as a great divide, but in the last half-century a series of bridges and tunnels has connected the nation together, culminating in the huge span constructed over the *Storebælt*. Today, automobiles and railways race across it in a few minutes. However, most people still think there are significant cultural differences between the Copenhagen-dominated east and the less densely populated west. Those on the Jutland peninsula are proud of their sturdy peasant background, and consider themselves to be down-to-earth, honest, hard-working people. To them, Copenhagen symbolizes high prices, snobbery, and extravagant living, particularly in the area north of the capital, which they derisively call, "the whiskey belt."

Those on the eastern side of the *Storebælt* claim that they alone speak Danish correctly, and tend to believe that they represent the nation's intellect and culture. They joke about the stupidity and narrowness of the people in Århus, which is Jutland's largest city, and complain about sending their soccer teams 'abroad' to play in Jutland.

Between Jutland and Zealand lies the island of Funen, sometimes called the garden of Denmark or the pearl of the Baltic. Its capital of Odense is the birthplace of Denmark's most famous writer, Hans Christian Andersen, and its most famous composer, Carl Nielsen. Its people claim to be musical, easy-going, and cheerful, though cynics point out that Andersen spent most of his life elsewhere. Finally, there is the region of South Jutland (*Sønderjylland*), bordering on Germany, which has a number of small cities, none dominant, and a dis-

The bridge over the Great Belt is larger than it looks. The Statue of Liberty could sit on the roadway and not reach the top.

tinctive dialect that disconcerts foreigners who thought they had mastered the Danish language.

While the geography of these regions is important, in cultural terms regional differences in Denmark are not as sharp as within Great Britain, Spain, or Italy, nor are they as politically important. More significant are the differences between thriving urban areas and isolated agricultural communities. Small islands, such as Ærø, Samsø, and Bornholm, attract tourists, yet locals feel the pinch of high unemployment, which would be even worse if many of the young had not left for jobs elsewhere. The government tries to keep these areas alive. It maintains daily mail service and ferry connections even to rather small islands that have only a few houses. Nevertheless, it has been difficult to keep communities alive in isolated places, and the vast majority of Danes now live in cities and towns, not small islands and farms.

Denmark west of the *Storebælt* has developed rapidly since 1945, to the point where it now contains half of the country's manufacturing industry. Between 1979 and 1989 the western regions increased modestly in population, despite out-migration from their rural areas, while the country as a whole did not experience any significant population growth. In contrast, Copenhagen shrank by 8%, partly because many moved into the countryside of central Zealand.

More recently, however, there has been something of a building boom in greater Copenhagen, which, with 1.34 million inhabitants, is larger than the next three largest cities combined (Århus, 274,000, Odense 181,000, and Ålborg, 158,000). It is not only the nation's capital, but serves as the center for finance, politics, and culture.

While the government has self-consciously tried to redress this imbalance between the capital and the rest of the nation, a disproportionate number of government jobs are located in and around Copenhagen.

Occasionally, a political party announces it wants to decentralize government, but in practice it proved impossible to move even the National Archives to a site 75 minutes away by regular train. Because of this persistent centralization, provincial areas at times rightly complain that their taxes are sucked into the Copenhagen's vast bureaucracy of office workers, with little advantage to themselves. Such complaints are hardly unique to Denmark, of course, and they have not led to the development of regionally based political parties.

Indeed, in terms of time, Denmark has shrunk during the last twenty years, as new high speed trains have cut travel time to and from Copenhagen by 50%. It has become common for workers to commute as much as halfway across the country. If jobs tend to be in the larger cities, homes increasingly may be almost anywhere. Indeed, another new bridge and tunnel system connects Copenhagen and Malmø in Sweden, making it an easy commute for the thousands who prefer its less expensive housing or the hundreds whose foreign spouse is still waiting for permission to live in Denmark.

The extensive Danish coastline made it a sea power for most of its history. The ocean long served as a protective barrier, and if a foreign army did invade, it proved difficult to subdue a country split into so many small parts. Aside from its natural protection, after 1700 Denmark was preserved as a small independent state in part by the foreign policies of England, France, and Russia, all of whom wanted to maintain free entry to the Baltic.

Nevertheless, the country became increasingly vulnerable to armies with modern technologies. Recognizing this fact, the Danish government stopped armed resistance a few hours after Germany's army, navy, and air force invaded on April 9, 1940. In practical terms, Denmark's enormous coastline remains difficult to defend against foreign attack. Russia briefly held Bornholm at the end of World War II, for example, but soon voluntarily gave it up. Now that Denmark is part of the EU, the coastline no longer needs defense in the same way. Instead, the country's extensive beaches have become a summer tourist attraction, not least because they are among the cleanest in Europe.

In terms of race and religion, Denmark long had one of the most homogeneous populations in the world. Until the 1960s almost all citizens were of Nordic stock, and most were members of the Lutheran Church, which they supported by taxes. A small Catholic minority and a few Protestant sects were fully tolerated, but they did not receive tax support. This homogeneity began to change when guest workers were imported due to a labor shortage. A steady stream of migrants and refugees followed,

The western coast of Jutland, with WW II bunker.

creating a more multicultural population, with political and social consequences discussed below.

The 'New Danes', as they are sometimes called, arrived in a largely secular society. For despite the Danish willingness to pay a special church tax, attendance at religious services is generally low except on high holy days. Interest in theology is weak. Even most university students cannot explain more than the most obvious literary references to the Bible. In short, most Danes are comfortable with the Lutheran label but not terribly interested in the details of their religion. Theological discussions are rare. The most obvious distinction they make among themselves is according to language. Regional accents pinpoint where each person is from, but social class is less marked by accent than in Great Britain.

Perhaps because Danes live in a small nation, they are curious about what lies beyond their borders. They are fond of traveling, and for centuries have been a seafaring country. Starting in the 1960s, they embraced one week charter vacations that took them all over Europe, particularly to warmer, sunnier places. It is hard to find a Dane who has not enjoyed the beaches of Spain or Greece. In recent decades, many have toured North America and the Orient as well. New Zealand and Australia also became popular well before 2004, when Crown Prince Frederick married a young woman from Tasmania. All in all, Danes remain outward looking and know a good deal about other nations and cultures.

Immigration

Despite their frequent travel, however, Danes have had some trouble adjusting psychologically to new immigrants coming to live amongst them, particularly those who come from outside Western Europe. Denmark was once a polyglot empire including much of the Baltic region, but in recent centuries homogeneity has become part of the national identity.

During the prosperous 1960s, there were few problems for the guest workers invited into the country. By definition, all had jobs on arrival, giving them an obvious right to pensions and welfare programs. Today, in contrast, many arrive as refugees and remain unemployed. In addition, it has sometimes proven difficult to assimilate people who have daily TV and Internet access to their homelands, particularly those who remain practicing Moslems.

Generalizations are difficult, however, since these 'New Danes' come from many different nations, including Turkey, Somalia, Palestine, Iraq, Bosnia, Vietnam, Iran, Pakistan, and many others. Those with a middle-class background are more likely to find work, get an education, or assimilate. But because the newer arrivals taken as a group are less likely to get work and more likely to receive welfare payments, this situation has become the source of political tension.

If immigrants are treated as equals when it comes to social services, most Danes take it for granted that they should assimilate fully. Indeed, new arrivals who receive welfare payments are required to attend Danish language classes. In practice, immigrants from Western Europe and the United States blend in sufficiently so that they are little noticed. This is far less likely for newcomers whose cultural differences are greater. Yet, whatever their background, the children of immigrants become more assimilated than their parents. Some have entered politics and sit in city councils and in the national assembly (the *Folketing*). Such integration is widely applauded. But the idea that immigrants have a right to retain and to cultivate their own culture is by no means universally accepted.

Indeed, The Danish People's Party has successfully pressed for tight controls to reduce the number of people migrating into the country. While the parties on the left reject extreme immigration restriction measures, many of their members also feel that it is unfair to give housing and the full range of social services to people who have just arrived. Danes know that in order to pay for these services their taxes are among the highest in the world. Some ask why newcomers who have never paid these taxes should receive all the benefits.

These concerns are reinforced by another problem: housing prices have doubled in the last decade, and it is hard for a young working couple in Copenhagen to find a place they can afford. Some of them ask if new immigrants really should get housing subsidies from the government. Yet it must be emphasized that on the whole most people are friendly to foreigners, and Danes pride themselves on being tolerant and hospitable people.

Class Structure

In Denmark it is not always easy to tell a person's social class. Dress is informal, language is rather uniform, and so many people speak foreign languages that the local baker may speak excellent English with a BBC accent and watch German television at night. Indeed, to the visitor it may appear that, although Denmark has a titled aristocracy, it has virtually abolished social classes. In most cities, it is hard to find anything resembling a slum, and the streets are clean and well kept. Medical care and education are free.

There seem to be few barriers to anyone seeking a career. Poverty is rare. People are protected by a safety net of services so extensive that no one should be homeless, although in practice a small number are, a few by choice. Consumer goods are widely available and well distributed. Virtually all Danes have television, radio, and mobile phones, and most also have Internet connections. Families can afford automobiles, although not all buy them, especially in Copenhagen, where an excellent public transit system makes cars less necessary. Indeed, a Dane can rise to the highest positions of authority without needing to know how to drive a car.

In 2009, the average Danish family had an income of 443.800 kroner, or about €59.000, before taxes. Furthermore, the difference between the top and the bottom is smaller than in any other industrial nation. The highest average family incomes, in suburbs near Copenhagen, were only slightly more than double the lowest average incomes in the poorest rural areas, and this was before taxes and high Copenhagen house prices further lessened the difference. Indeed, in 2005 people in rural Jutland had more money to spend per capita on Christmas presents than the people in Copenhagen.

The way families spend their income has changed considerably in the last thirty years, as real incomes have increased. In 1974, 28% of Danish consumption went for tobacco, beverages, and food; in 2004 that figure had dropped to only 16%. Money has shifted into buying housing, heat, and electricity, which now takes almost a third of disposable income. The cost of transport has also been increasing. Yet overall, even if spending has shifted its emphasis, Denmark is an egalitarian society. One's first impression can easily be that the country's only real problem is too much bureaucracy.

Putting all this on the plus side, however, there are some negative aspects to the Danish system. Women consistently earn less than men, and only 20% of those making more than 500,000 kroner a year are female. At the other end of the spectrum, only 40% of those making less than 250,000 kroner are men. In addition, critics have argued that Danish taxes are regressive, placing a relatively heavier burden on workers and the middle class than on the wealthy.

Are there rich people in Denmark? A union organization complained in 1983 that 10% of the population held 55% of the wealth, and noted that when direct and indirect taxes were added together, there was virtually no difference between the tax rate of the wealthy and the poor. Moreover, class distinctions apparently are becoming sharper. In 1991, the national newspaper *Politiken* reported that the top tenth of the population owned 75% of the taxable goods. In 2002 a study found that despite universal stipends for higher education, children of workers were far less likely to complete university than those from the middle class.

Those at the bottom of Danish society are certainly better off than the poor in most countries, but their chances of climbing to a higher class level are modest. If education is free, entrance to the university is not automatic, but depends on a student's grades in gymnasium (high school). In some subjects less than half the applicants are admitted. Families who are better off can give their children various forms of cultural enrichment such as a summer abroad to perfect language skills, which gives them a competitive edge in seeking admission.

In short, Denmark has tried to maximize equality and it appears to be homogeneous, but class divisions do exist, and they tend to be reproduced from one generation to the next.

The Family

Families are important in every society, but perhaps no where more so than in Denmark. Nevertheless, most Danish nuclear families are small. Few have more than two children, although in recent years some couples have begun to have three, and the birthrate has begun to rise from an all time low of only 1.4 per female in 1983 to 1.7 – although a rate of 2.1 is necessary to keep the population constant. Labor law encourages families to have children, as it permits either the father or the mother a leave of absence from work, with pay, for six months each time a child is born. In addition, families with children receive "child money" (*børnepenge*), or tax-free payments from the state to help pay the cost of rearing each child.

Furthermore, every city and town subsidizes child care centers where parents can leave pre-schoolers during working hours. Three out of four small children are placed in these centers every weekday. As this might suggest, three out of four women work. In recent years sex roles have also begun to change, and men have taken on more duties in the home. Yet, even with leave of absence during pregnancy, child payments, subsidized daycare and other incentives, the old-stock Danish population is not managing to replace itself. Detailed knowledge of birth control is widespread, and many women avoid getting pregnant.

But there is roughly one voluntary abortion for every four live births. Despite the low birthrate, however, the population is growing, due to longer life expectancy, immigration, and a high birthrate among immigrants. Because of these developments, the profile of the population is changing. There are more old people and fewer youngsters. There are more sons and daughters of immigrants, but fewer children overall. The number of people on pensions is growing, while the number of workers whose taxes can support them is shrinking. Future politicians will need to be creative to resolve these contradictions. However, it is unlikely that they will try to legislate a new national morality.

Danes are informal about marriage, and do not think it is necessary before people live together. You can meet couples in any social class that have lived together for years and had children without bothering to get married. Nearly half of all infants are born out of wedlock, but this does not mean they lack loving parents. Neither Danish law nor the tax code strongly encourages formal marriage, and only a minority feel they must marry for religious reasons. Civil ceremonies in the town hall that last only a few minutes are common, and they cost virtually nothing.

There is little social pressure to get married, and a couple that chooses to do so often has lived together for years. Nevertheless, when it occurs, a wedding is usually a big event, with a full day devoted to the ceremony, reception, dinner, and dancing that lasts long into the night. Starting in 1989 Danish law permitted people of the same sex to marry in a civil ceremony. While some Lutheran ministers objected at the time, there is no controversy about the matter today.

It would be mistaken to conclude, based on marriage patterns, that the family is an unimportant institution. On the contrary, married or not, Danes spend much of their leisure time with the family. On weekends and holidays, especially in smaller communities, the visitor is often astonished to find the streets empty, as though everyone had evacuated the area. Don't be alarmed, the Danes have merely retreated into the privacy of their homes. On a typical Sunday, the roads are largely empty of traffic and few shops are open, as most Danes spend much of the day with their parents and children.

Given the high expectations for a happy nuclear family, some are disappointed and the divorce rate is high. Many Danes search for a new partner and remarry, affirming the family's importance. But many end up alone. About one quarter of all Danes live by themselves, including a good many pensioners and most students.

Language

It is far easier to learn to read Danish than to speak it. Compared to most other languages, the consonants are less emphatic and the vowels are more numerous. Indeed, there are so many vowel sounds in Danish that it requires three extra letters in the alphabet (æ, ø, and å) to help express them. (A practical pointer: When using Danish telephone books and dictionaries, note that these three extra vowels are at the end of the alphabet. A word beginning with Å is not found in the front, but at the back of the book.) Some of the vowel sounds come from deep in the throat — the kinds of sounds your parents probably taught you not to make.

It takes time to distinguish one guttural noise from another, not to mention some courage to try to reproduce them. To make matters even worse, the length of a vowel also matters. For example, the Danish words for "bird" and "drunk" sound the same, except for the length of time you spend articulating the vowel. Shortly after arrival, someone will probably ask you to pronounce *rødgrød med fløde,* the name of a dessert that roughly means red fruit porridge with cream. It is virtually impossible for a non-native to say this correctly, although you *may* find that you like to eat it.

It is advisable to begin learning Danish before arrival, for it is hardly a language that can be picked up in a few months. Knowledge of the other Scandinavian languages or German will be helpful in acquiring a good vocabulary. Danish pronunciation is quite another matter, as the spoken language does not closely correspond to the written form. Swedes say a Dane sounds like he has a throat disease and a potato in his mouth. I have heard Swedes switch over to English because they cannot understand a Danish bank cashier.

Fortunately for readers of this booklet, except for those who wish to learn the language, almost all Danes speak some English and they like to practice. (The only apparent exceptions are old railway conductors, taxi drivers with a foreign background, and the government officials whom you absolutely must communicate with.)

Often it seems that Danes find it so tiring to speak their own language that, to relax their throats, they prefer to switch to other European languages. In addition to English, which is the principle second language, many know Swedish or German, both from school and from television.

A good many also have an acquaintance with one of the romance languages. This multi-lingual competence is enhanced by the policy of broadcasting television shows and films in the original language, with sub-titles instead of dubbing. This also benefits the visiting foreigners, in turn, who can learn some Danish vocabulary by reading sub-titles. Watching American and British television programs, regardless of their quality, need not be time lost from cultural immersion, if you remember to read the bottom of the screen too.

Cultural Influence from Abroad

Compared with the rest of the world, Norway, Sweden, and Denmark appear similar. When viewed close-up, however, the three countries seem quite distinct, with the greatest cultural distance between Denmark and Sweden, while Norway lies between them. Rather than speak of influence from one Scandinavian country to another, it might be more accurate to say that each relies on the others to retain a common sense of identity.

The day-to-day cultural influence of these neighbors is continuous, if not always obvious. Some parts of Denmark receive Swedish or Norwegian television, of course, and together the three countries share a common airline, SAS, and a number of cultural institutions. Indeed, there are councils that provide funding for joint cultural ventures, such as academic journals, conferences, and literary events. Art museums often hold exhibitions featuring Scandinavian works, and each year some novels from one nation are best-sellers in the other countries. This does not mean that the these nations are converging in a common culture.

The languages and traditions remain quite distinct. Rather, like France and Italy or Spain and Portugal, these nations are close enough to take pleasure in the nuances of small differences and are able to engage in considerable depth and detail the richness of neighboring cultures. In this exchange, it should be emphasized that Finland has a language that almost no one in Denmark understands, and it is distinctly further away in its mentality and culture. Denmark, Norway, and Sweden make up Scandinavia. Add Finland and Iceland and the proper term is the Nordic Countries.

In tracing the influence of non-Nordic nations in Denmark, it is best to make a broad distinction between popular and high culture. Popular culture is strongly influenced by American and British sources, notably television, films, rock music, and the Internet. Most Danes have seen Will and Grace, Desperate Housewives, and the Academy Awards. They know the lyrics to many British rock songs, and have read a considerable amount of mass-market fiction, both in English and in translation. In a typical year, two-thirds of the 2000 books translated into Danish come from the English-speaking world.

In the fine arts, however, other European cultures are more important. France, Spain, and Italy provide the wines Danes prefer to drink and the foreign food they prefer to eat, and these nations plus Germany provide the orchestral music Danes prefer to hear, the philosophical systems they prefer to think with, and the political systems closest to their own. The feeling toward Germany is complex, of course, because of the loss of Slesvig-Holsten in the nineteenth century and the German occupation during World War II. As Denmark's most powerful neighbor, it cannot help but exert a constant cultural and economic pressure. Since the reunification of Germany and the collapse of the Soviet sphere, there has also been a quickening of Danish interest in central Europe. Overall, the strongest foreign cultural and political impulses certainly come from within the European Union.

When considering the English-speaking world, some Danes prefer BBC English to American pronunciation, and think of London as the cultural center. This is logical enough, since it is cheaper and faster to visit London than New York. Likewise, Britain is more likely to offer political inspiration, while American politics is commonly held up to scorn. (In a 2004 poll, Danes overwhelmingly preferred John Kerry, Ralph Nadar came in second, and George Bush received less than 5%.)

Yet, if many appreciate British theater, follow British politics, read the latest London best sellers, and relish British humor, Danes have taken an increasing interest in American popular culture, which seems to them an exotic mix of personal freedom, informality, creativity, extreme wealth and poverty, glittering skylines, crime, oppression, African-American struggle, circus-like elections, rock and roll, religious fanaticism, the Wild West, and rags-to-riches success. In short, Great Britain has traditionally represented cultural sophistication, while the United States is often seen as exciting but distinctly lowbrow. A surprising number of Danes have been to Australia, which combines a familiar language with an exotic natural world, and whose bright summer coincides with the dreary Baltic winter.

When looking at international affairs, Danes see the world from the vantage point of a small nation. In conversation people often say, "But we are a small country," an expression meant to cover a multitude of differences. Denmark does not have the illusion, so common to large nations, that it is a self-sufficient entity. Danes are acutely aware that neighboring countries and world powers affect their political, economic, and ecological welfare. This realization at times stirs some resentment, and it may also explain why Danes almost instinctively sympathize with other small nations, ethnic minorities, and develop-

The alternative society of Christiania.

ing countries whose political and cultural continuity is precarious.

Danes are likely to look with some suspicion on the motives of all the great powers in the international arena, even if on the whole they usually side with Western Europe. (See the section of Politics, below.) Likewise, perhaps because Danes live at the boundary between Scandinavia and the rest of Europe and at the meeting point between eastern and western Europe, they try to see all sides to an issue. Certainly, they never shared the virulent anti-communism found in some other western countries.

In thinking about the larger world, Danes strive for a balanced view and maintain their cultural independence. Nor have they been overwhelmed by globalization. If they hear a good deal of foreign popular music, they also have a wealth of home-grown talent, and many of the songs on the radio and in their top ten list were recorded locally. Likewise, Danish authors and filmmakers manage to hold their own, and occasionally become international themselves. It would be a serious error for the visitor to assume that Danish culture is just a partial copy of what they already know, or to assume that it is inexorably being homogenized by market forces. In short, the Danes have a distinctive culture that is evolving in its own way.

National Character

Egalitarians?

For many visitors, Danish social solidarity is an inspiring example, compared to the individualism and inequality of many western societies. By taxing automobiles heavily, they can afford well-coordinated collective transport. By keeping income taxes high, they can provide good social services, free medical care, and free university education. Historically speaking, these social services are the result of a wide range of factors. In the nineteenth century, the nation developed strong trade unions and witnessed a powerful religious and educational reform movement. Both contributed to the emergence of twentieth century social democratic governments that created the welfare state.

Yet, there is also a less happy side to the national mentality that created this egalitarian system. No one can live long in Denmark without hearing the term *janteloven*.

This means "the law of Jante," and was first coined in 1933 by the Danish writer Aksel Sandemose in a novel that took place in Jante, a small Norwegian town. All Danes can quote a line or two from the Jante law, whose ten commandments, if followed, would create an unchanging, collective mentality.

1. Thou shalt not believe thou art something.
2. Thou shalt not believe thou art as good as we.
3. Thou shalt not believe thou art more wise than we.
4. Thou shalt not fancy thyself better than we.
5. Thou shalt not believe thou knowest more than we.
6. Thou shalt not believe thou art greater than we.
7. Thou shalt not believe thou amountest to anything.
8. Thou shalt not laugh at us.
9. Thou shalt not believe that anyone is concerned with thee.
10. Thou shalt not believe thou canst teach us anything.

In the Jante law egalitarianism takes an extreme form, and many say it goes too far. Yet, until at least the 1980s or half a century after Sandemose published them, these attitudes dominated the nation's mentality. Danes insisted that people should not consider themselves better than their fellows, and they usually put on the appearance of modesty if they won an award or published a book.

Students who received an award seldom bragged about it. One television commercial from the end of this period caught the mentality perfectly, by depicting a man who had just won a large sum of money in the national lottery. In most nations a person blessed with such good luck would celebrate immediately, jumping for joy and quite likely shouting. But such behavior would be contrary to the Jante law. Instead, the man repressed his feelings, ran

Detail from Danish artist Bjørn Nørgaard's 17 pieces of tapestry for Her Majesty the Queen of Denmark.

down into a subway station, and waited patiently for a train to come rumbling in. Only then, when the train came to a screeching halt and no one could hear him, did he jump and shout for joy. Such a lottery advertisement would not have made sense in Italy or England. Indeed, it now seems a little dated in Denmark as well.

Danes long have expected people to behave as equals, perhaps especially if they are not. For example, many patients resent it if a doctor acts as though his profession puts him above them. In some important ways such values supported social equality, as in the educational system. Perhaps the most striking example of Danish social solidarity came in World War II, when they refused to allow the Germans to deport the 6,000 Danish Jews. Instead, they organized an extraordinary underground action in which they managed to save all but 550, ferrying the rest to safety in neutral Sweden.

Yet, in recent years many Danes have begun to attack the whole idea of the Jante law. It may be suited to emergencies and times of crisis, and it may help maintain social solidarity, but it also stifles individual initiative and self-reliance, and it can lead to narrowness and blind adherence to custom. For these reasons, some people on the political right have openly rejected it, including one businessman whose slogan was "Break the Jante law." (Many, however, found this slogan disgustingly egotistical.)

On the left side of the spectrum, where the Jante law traditionally had enjoyed much support, other problems arose. By definition, the Jante law cannot value ethnic diversity or underwrite the idea of a multicultural society. In short, the consensus that Danish society could be described by the Jante law has broken down, although nothing has clearly emerged to take its place.

Leadership

Danish leadership differs from that in many other countries. Even if the Jante law is less pervasive than before, still a Danish leader does not want to seem overbearing or dominant, but rather to express the will of the group. Passionate speeches are rare, disarming jokes are common. Not surprisingly, high-handed and dictatorial approaches antagonize most Danes, who respond better when someone appeals to the common good. If you attend a meeting where important decisions must be made, be prepared for a long affair with a great deal of talk. In contrast to Anglo-American meetings, most speakers will avoid the word "I," using the first person plural "we" as much as possible. They will appeal to earlier agreements and decisions, suggesting continuities with successful policies. In other words, they seek to speak for the group, not for themselves alone. Danes prefer not to vote at all if they can achieve consensus through a long discussion.

Ordinary British or American procedures, such as putting a motion on the floor, seconding the motion, debating it, and calling for a vote on the question, are virtually unknown, no doubt because they are divisive. Danes debate with the object of winning everyone to their position, and they seldom try to score points against one another personally. They dislike any procedure in a meeting that forces them openly to take sides. A stranger sitting in a long meeting will often be startled to see that, after interminable discussion, the final vote is unanimous.

In part, people almost never wish to stand out alone against the group. Even when a clear division does exist, they may publicly deny it. If differences are really intractable, they may postpone action until consensus can be achieved at another meeting. In the Danish *Folketing*, where votes are unavoidable, most important decisions are made in closed meetings within each party, who then hold discussions with one another, with the goal of reaching an agreement beforehand. In the legislature itself, the Prime Minister usually only takes a measure to a vote if a majority has been assembled beforehand. Dramatic ballots where the outcome is uncertain are rare, because party discipline is much stronger than in many other parliaments. In short, because the goal is consensus, legislative sessions often are drained of passion, and the unexpected is unlikely.

The Daily Round

In most situations, Danes waste few moments in pleasantries, rituals, or formalities. When acquaintances pass in the street, they may exchange only a single word of greeting or perhaps just nod their heads to one another without breaking stride. Withdrawing money from the bank or going to the post office, one stands in line, has a rapid exchange with the teller, and moves on to the next task, usually without getting into conversation with others waiting in line.

Likewise, on buses or other public transportation, a large group of passengers may ride in almost complete silence. But note that all these encounters are between strangers. Danes are not quiet when together with friends. A group traveling on a bus or train will be talkative, even loud. Likewise, the speed of transactions slows down when people know one another. Drop into the office of an acquaintance and he or she usually offers a cup of coffee or other refreshments. Even if you have but the briefest business, the visit will often turn into a short meeting. It is important not to refuse the offered hospitality, and if at all possible do not rush the occasion.

The rhythm of daily life varies considerably according to the weather. During the dark winters, Danes remain mostly inside. Indoor entertainment from September until May is excellent, including regular performances by the many state-supported symphony orchestras, theaters, the Royal Ballet, and The Royal Opera, now in a stun-

The new opera house in Copenhagen.

ning new building reflected in the Copenhagen harbor. Due to subsidies, tickets are reasonably priced, and much cheaper than similar high-quality fare in Paris, New York, or London. The most common winter sports are also indoor activities: badminton, ice hockey on artificial rinks, basketball, soccer, and indoor team handball. The Danish women's handball team has won a huge national following, because it has been one of the best in the world in recent years, winning both the world championship and Olympic gold medals.

Until the late 1980s the Danish state had a monopoly on television, and operated only one channel, with no advertising allowed. Its broadcast day began in the late afternoon and ended by midnight. Since then commercial Danish TV stations have proliferated, programming has expanded to fill the day, and advertising fills every permitted pause. Daytime television is as boring as anywhere else, but in the evening networks carry a wide variety of programs, including concerts and interviews with authors as well as films and popular entertainment. Most homes are equipped with cable or satellite dishes, and receive 30 or more stations from the rest of Europe, with the result that there is always something on in both English and German, and usually in other major languages as well. Indeed, many cable systems routinely provide programming in Turkish. Broadband Internet hookups are also becoming quite common, and one is unlikely to feel cut off from the rest of the world.

When the days lengthen in the spring, people immediately find a reason to go outside if the weather is sunny. They garden, cycle, and loiter, or simply take long walks. Don't be surprised if women sunbathe topless on the beaches, in city parks, or at a summer rock concert. Danes are not upset by public nudity. Entertainment generally moves outside, notably including the Copenhagen Jazz festival in early summer, outdoor theater performances, and open-air rock concerts, such as the one in Roskilde that takes place near the end of June. Generally, from about June 25 until August 10, life slows to a crawl, as Danish families take their vacations. (Indeed,

Don't be surprised if women are topless at the beach.

they are required by law to take six weeks off during each year, even if they are unemployed.) Most offices are understaffed, some factories close, and the universities are virtually empty, as there is little tradition for holding summer school. The rhythm picks up sharply again in the first week of August, when children go back to school. If one is planning to spend a year in Denmark, it is well to note that in social terms a new year begins in August more than on January 1.

The workday begins early — many are on the job by eight in the morning, most are there by nine — and it also ends early. By 6:00 in the evening most shops are closed and people are at home. Supermarkets and some bakeries remain open somewhat longer. A small local store may stay open as late as 10 PM, but after that the only places to buy cigarettes or milk are the all night gas stations. On Friday a lot of shops stay open until about 7:30, and many people are out. Saturday morning is one of the busiest times in the week, until two or at most four in the afternoon, when by law most shops must close down. The main streets in Danish towns are virtually deserted by the early evening, except for the center of Copenhagen. Where have the Danes gone?

Housing

Danes spend a great deal of time at home, and they invest large sums in furniture and design. Having nice furniture and a sleek new kitchen are high priorities, and for some people they come before owning a car. Even university students spend a surprising amount of time and money creating a comfortable home life. Like the rest of the population, they often prefer to live alone when not in a relationship. Having roommates is not common. Nevertheless, despite the high priority given to privacy and the home, Danes have done a worse job in supplying housing than might be expected. Almost 40% of its housing stock is from before 1940 (compared to 25% in Sweden), and new housing construction has not been particularly vigorous, although suburbs in some small cities are growing, notably Sorø, Ringsted, Faaborg, Køge, and Kerteminde. Government tax policies that once made home ownership relatively easy eventually cost so much in lost revenue that they had to be changed. Today, Danes can only write off about one-third of the interest on their mortgages.

On the bright side, however, interest rates have been historically low in recent years. Indeed, many families buy not only a house but a small apartment for a child at university. Demand is so high that there is chronic shortage of inexpensive housing in urban areas. Rented apartments seldom need to be advertised, as word of mouth is sufficient to attract lodgers. In Copenhagen, the problems with housing policy are the most obvious, and rents remain the highest in the country, but other cities have similar problems, notably Århus.

Socializing

Someone once said that a Dane is like a bottle of ketchup — at first nothing comes out, and then everything comes out at once. Friendship takes time, as Danes cultivate a few close friends, not a crowd of acquaintances. They do not seek ways to bring large heterogeneous groups together. For them, the cocktail party, the big picnic, or the wide-open party are not particularly common occurrences, though not as rare as a generation ago. Most Danes are uncomfortable and shy at large gatherings

In recent years cafés have been replacing pubs.

of strangers. While in recent years they have begun to patronize cafés instead of bars, they do not have a café society, in which adults customarily meet friends at their public haunts rather than at home. Young people, in contrast, frequent the bars and cafés, often until quite late at night, locating one another with their ubiquitous portable telephones.

Many outsiders who are long-term residents complain that Denmark is too private, too controlled, too ordered, and too ritualized. They feel it lacks spontaneity and could use a little anarchy. The ideal Danish evening consists of a long dinner at home with a group of friends who know one another well. There is a special term for such intimate occasions, which also can be applied to other cozy situations: *hyggelig*. It is *hyggeligt* to light a few candles, listen to classical music and chat over a cup of coffee with a few friends, or to sit in a secluded nook of a restaurant long after the food has been consumed, talking and having an after-dinner drink.

Meals

Food and drink represent about one fifth of total private consumption. Meals occur with almost clock-like regularity. Breakfast is eaten before 8 AM, almost always at home. A visitor who decides to go out for breakfast will not find cafés catering to a morning crowd, and there are no pancake houses. A few bakeries sell coffee, but they seldom provide a place to sit down. Only hotels and central railroad stations offer a real breakfast. Danes seldom eat fried food in the morning, preferring bread and cheese, yoghurt, and the like, plus coffee, which they drink more than tea. They like their coffee two ways: strong and often.

Lunch, or *frokost,* is at noon, and this is seldom a long or formal affair. Most people bring food with them to work in little square plastic boxes that fit neatly into briefcases and knapsacks. Universities and work places usually have canteens serving the cold open-faced sandwiches (called *smørrebrød*) that Danes prefer in the middle of the day. Outside central Copenhagen, relatively few people go to a restaurant to eat *frokost,* except for business people on expense accounts.

Dinner, somewhat confusingly called *middag,* is the only time-consuming meal, both in terms of preparation and consumption. Danes eat some fish, but most seem to prefer well-cooked meat and potatoes, served with an appropriate gravy or sauce. In recent years, as in other countries on the Continent, a lighter cuisine has also become popular. It is not unusual for Danes to linger over this meal for an hour, followed by the television news.

The summer music festival at Skanderborg.

On special occasions — and not just among the wealthy, but in most families — the evening meal lengthens into a five hour sit-down dinner with several courses, that typically starts at 7 in the evening. If there are many guests, each is assigned to a specific seat, where they are expected to remain throughout the meal. Toasts and after-dinner speeches take up a good deal of the time, and foreigners may find these occasions hard to get through. Americans, used to informality, may be charmed for the first two hours or so, but then become increasingly restless in their chairs during the next three. A Spanish woman at one such affair, who understood no Danish, after the fourth hour began muttering incessantly under her breath, "I am going to die."

Those who can understand what is going on, however, usually find these occasions light-hearted and relaxed — not least because at the table Danes seldom blend work and pleasure. People are invited not because of business, but because they are relatives and friends, and the common reference points are personal, not commercial.

Guests may compose songs for birthdays or holidays, and at weddings or other particularly important occasions there are skits, pantomimes, and even short plays. The next time a Dane sees someone whom he has invited home to dinner, he expects them to say "Tak for sidst," which means thank you for the last get-together. Even if the first encounter occurs several weeks after the dinner, most people remember to say these words, and it is considered bad form – even rude – to forget.

Evenings Out

When Danes go out in the evening, it is usually not to a bar, café, or restaurant, but to an activity. Evening courses in everything from languages to samba dancing are state-subsidized, and are available for modest prices. A good way to get to know the Danes is to take a non-credit course in something you are interested in. An outsider can best get to know people through such group activities. In contrast, do not expect to go into a restaurant or café and get into long conversations with strangers. There is no equivalent to the English neighborhood pub.

Many Danes go out as a group, often after doing something together earlier in the evening, such as hearing a talk, going to a workout, or rehearsing in a choir. Because people meet each other through group activities, there is less dating than in some other countries. Couples only pair off after they have already grown to know each other as part of a larger constellation. If you telephone a Dane and suggest going to the movies alone together, he or she may agree to it, but don't be surprised if they suggest meeting you at the theater. Going out alone with a new acquaintance is somewhat contrary to local custom, and it is more common for groups of people to socialize together.

When Danes go out, they seldom buy a round of drinks for a group. People usually pay their own way, and when you see the prices, you'll see why. Note that most Danish women work full time and they usually insist on paying for themselves. Put another way, Danish men do not expect to pay for a woman's theater tickets, food, and drink. In addition, helping a woman with her coat, holding the door for her, or other polite customs are not automatically observed, though they are usually appreciated.

"Old Danish" is an acquired taste.

Alcohol

Alcohol is more easily available in Denmark than in the other Nordic countries. It is sold in gas stations, supermarkets, department stores, vending machines, and railway stations. Long a beer-drinking nation, since joining the European Community Denmark has shifted about half its consumption to wine. A wide variety is available. In all but the cheapest restaurants, the wine list begins at more than 150 kroner (c. €20) per bottle. Be sure to try the many varieties of Danish beer, including the special brews made during the fall harvest, Christmas, and Easter, as well as the powerful *elephant* beer. The range on offer has increased in recent years, as some micro-breweries have emerged. You might also sample Gammel Dansk ("Old Danish"), a bitter dram taken in small quantities, which is a Danish specialty. It is sometimes served at breakfast — for most foreigners it is at best an acquired taste. The best tactic, if you cannot avoid Gammel Dansk, it is to take down a shot of it in one gulp.

In the evening, you may occasionally see Danes out for a stroll who are a little tipsy. Visitors need not be uneasy if they see a boisterous group approaching, for such people seldom become quarrelsome or violent. In general, it is reasonably safe to walk about at night in Denmark, and there are often people about until after ten in the evening. Likewise, sporting events are seldom attended by violence, though at the largest events the police are out in force, just in case. Danish football (soccer) fans have explicitly rejected hooliganism, defining themselves as *roligans*—a term derived from the Danish word for peaceful (*rolig*). As a result, they are popular visitors all over Europe, as is their national team, which won the European championship in 1992 and often qualifies for the World Cup, though not in 2006.

Danes pride themselves on being Roligans (peaceful fans).

Smoking

As recently as a decade ago foreigners found Danish smoking habits twenty years behind the times. Many adults smoked everywhere without apology or any sense that it might be offensive to others. Even hospitals had designated smoking areas. Today, in contrast, smoking has been banned from public buildings and restaurants.

Bars are also smoke-free, though some of them may provide a separate room for smokers. Concern about passive smoking has become widespread, and recently the cigarette packages have been forced to display disturbing photographs of medical conditions that can be caused by using tobacco. While cigars and cigarettes are costly, however, they can be purchased in many places.

The Educational System

Required primary school (*folkeskole*) in Denmark begins at age 7, though 90% of all children start their education with two years of optional kindergarten. State policy dictates that gifted children should not be singled out for special attention or put into separate groups, because it is thought to be desireable that all sorts of students learn to get along with one another.

At the completion of *folkeskole* at age 16 or 17, students decide whether to enter state vocational training schools, which offer a long and thorough training, or to compete for admission to three years of more advanced study at the gymnasium-level. If they select the last option, they then must decide whether to focus on business, science, or the humanities. The grades given during this three year education are crucial, because the over-all average is the chief criterion used for admission to the university level.

The choices available at this point are as varied as anywhere in Western Europe, with many quite separate institutions involved. Universities offer degrees in the humanities, social sciences, science and medicine, but nurses are trained in hospitals. Teacher training and the fine arts such as painting, design, and music have their own institutions. There have been many more foreign students in Denmark in recent years and an increasing number of courses offered in English to accommodate them. Danes apply to university in the spring and find out where they have been accepted during the summer. About two-thirds of all applicants are admitted, though not necessarily to the program that was their first choice. Selectivity varies considerably by department, and the government does impose quotas on some areas. Once admitted, students study their major field almost exclusively. Partly because the choice of subject, once made, is not easily changed, after gymnasium more than half of all students take a year or more off before continuing their studies. Many use this time to travel or to work abroad. As a result, first year students at university are twenty or older, and noticeably more mature than in England or the United States.

Danish students pay no tuition, and for up to six years they are eligible for state stipends that help to pay for books and living expenses. Unfortunately, this generosity does not extend to the university system as a whole. Sweden invests more per student than Denmark, which in recent years has weakened financial support for university education, despite political rhetoric about the importance of education and research in the emerging information society. Because universities have almost no endowment and are not allowed to charge tuition, they are far more dependent on state funding than in many other nations. When support falters or fluctuates they cannot temporarily fall back on their own resources, but must make drastic cuts instead.

There is less student life at business schools and universities in Denmark than most foreigners are accustomed to. Danes have chosen not to make the university a separate enclave in society, with its own way of life. Foreign students are usually surprised to find that few sports facilities are available to Danish students, and that the only common meeting places are canteens, which do not have a large selection. At four in the afternoon, all the offices close, and shortly afterward the telephone switchboard, the library, and the canteen also close, leaving little reason for anyone to remain at the university. As a result, students often seize the chance to socialize at school during the day, doing all their work at home during the evening.

Danish universities or business schools are not designed to accommodate hundreds of students studying on campus. For those who want to read for an hour or two between classes, quiet nooks and study halls are often hard to find and libraries are small and can be noisy. The rhythm of campus life is dictated by the administrative staff, who work by the clock, quitting at four or five every day, except on Fridays when offices close earlier. Usually the buildings are deserted by late afternoon, except for a few adult education students. On holidays and weekends, university outside doors are usually locked.

As this suggests, Danish universities are less residential and more commuter campuses. Some students live at home. Dormitories are spread around town, dispersing the students into small groups. There is no dining commons attached to the residence halls; rather students shop for and prepare their own food. This arrangement makes Danish student life rather private. Indeed, virtually all students have single rooms. On evenings or weekends, entertainment, whether in the form of sports, eating, reading, or seeing other people, seldom takes place at the university.

Social life is almost invisible to outsiders, but occurs in student rooms and apartments. Those who want exercise join a sports club or gym; musicians audition for choirs and orchestras. Of course, there are clusters of bars and inexpensive restaurants frequented by students, but on the whole, there is no sharp division between town and gown. If there is little student life, there is also no student ghetto.

Daily life in advanced educational institutions focuses largely on individual departments. Until recently, little attempt was made to facilitate contact between different fields of study. Cross-registration between schools is becoming more common but it is often hard to arrange. Students are admitted to study in one field, and after the first days at the university they may seldom have contact with people in other fields. Foreign students do not enter a vast anonymous university; rather they come to know a relatively small cluster of people who can be found in the same places from day to day.

Academic life focuses at the local level; there are almost no occasions – such as sporting events, rock concerts, or symposia – where one feels part of the whole university. Indeed, Danish universities usually have only one yearly ceremony, called *årsfest*. Only a fraction of faculty and students are able to attend, however, because there are no rooms large enough to seat more than a few hundred people. Nothing indicates more clearly the fragmented nature of Danish higher education than the lack of graduation ceremonies. There is a collective celebration each year when students complete the gymnasium, but university departments may do little to mark the end of the academic year. Students often disappear one by one as they finish.

Another important educational institution must also be emphasized: the folk high schools. Founded in the nineteenth century as part of an idealistic reform movement, these popular voluntary schools are dedicated to education for its own sake, not as a means to an end. Usually located in rural or island settings, they are residential, admitting students of all ages for courses in a wide variety of subjects. In recent years, however, the government has reduced funding for the folk high schools and a few have closed. Yet, they remain a vital part of Danish life, and they are an excellent place for a foreigner to gain insight into the culture.

Economics and Politics

Trade and the Economy

Denmark has one of the more successful economies in the EU. During the economic crisis that began in 2008, its unemployment remained much lower than in most of Europe and investors regarded the Danish kroner as a safe haven. When the World Bank ranked 130 nations, it found Denmark to be number eight for its overall ease of doing business. This was higher than any other EU nation, just ahead of Britain (9th) and Ireland (11th), and a much better showing than Germany (19th), Spain (30th), or Italy (70th). In part, this success is due to a good national work ethic, a passion for order, a low level of corruption, and to a general pride in making things work efficiently. But such success depends on far more. Denmark has long been an important trading nation, with fleets of merchant ships sailing around the world. The same survey found Denmark number one in the world for ease of trade across borders and number two (just after Norway) in the enforcement of contracts. Clearly, it is well-organized, safe, and efficient. Danish geography no doubt encourages trade, as the nation stands at the crossroads of the Baltic. Indeed, Copenhagen, translated, means "merchant harbor." Today, a great deal of shipping also flows through Esbjerg and Århus on Jutland, and the largest port in the country is Fredericia. Since 1987 there has been a trade surplus in every year, often as high as 4% of GDP.

Fully 70% of this trade is with the EU, almost half with Germany and Sweden. About 5% of total trade is with the United States and Canada, 4% with China, and smaller amounts with a large number of other nations. These figures only give a partial picture of the Danish role in world trade, however, because Danish firms also engage in extensive ship building and operate a number of shipping companies. Furthermore, income increasingly derives from foreign subdivisions, overseas investments, banking, fees, transfers, and other services.

While often perceived as a chiefly agricultural country, Denmark is highly industrialized. Only 5% of the population still live on farms, and many of these farmers would disappear without EU subsidies. There is little mining compared to the other Nordic countries, but the oil and natural gas extraction industries supply all the nation's needs and more. One of Denmark's largest companies, and certainly the most visible, is Carlsberg, which sells beer worldwide. But overall, the economy is diversified, quite unlike Sweden, which has several companies that are among the world's 500 largest corporations. Notably,

Denmark is a leading windmill producer.

Denmark has no automobile plants and few assembly-line industries. Indeed, compared to most European countries, it has little heavy industry, which on the whole is probably an advantage.

There are a few large companies, of course, such as A. P. Møller (a conglomerate emphasizing shipping, transport, supermarkets, and oil), Novo Nordisk (pharmaceuticals), and Lego (toys), but most Danes work for companies with less than 200 employees. In recent years, some Danish companies have merged in order to compete more successfully in the European Union. For example, two of the largest pharmaceuticals, six of the largest banks, and all of the major meat packers have undergone mergers. Even so, most companies are still small by international standards.

Gross national product has grown steadily since 1990, while inflation has averaged less than 2% a year. Since Danish wages are high – the minimum is about €14.50 an hour, plus standard benefits such as pensions and five weeks of vacation – companies cannot compete in mass production. Rather they specialize where high quality and reliability are imperative. For example, Danish companies produce 40% of the world's hearing aids, two-thirds of the world's pre-insulated pipes, and a rather amazing 50% of the world's seeds, including an even higher percentage of organic seeds.

Luxury goods are also an important part of Danish exports, notably porcelain, furniture, and furs. About 100 factories produce stylish wooden furniture annually worth $700 million. Likewise, 2200 Danish breeders produce 40% of the world's mink. Other companies specialize in such things as the manufacture of hospital equipment, computer software, vending machines, turn-key dairies, and pollution control equipment. By focusing in such areas and spreading their investments in many smaller companies, Danes have built up one of the most diversified and strongest economies in Europe, with an extensive safety-net of social services that justify its high tax rate.

Energy

In part, Danish economic success also rests on a better energy supply than most European Community nations. When it began to exploit its reserves of oil and gas in the North Sea thirty years ago, about 10% of Danish imports were oil. Today, 5% of the exports are oil. Likewise, as late as 1981 little natural gas was used in the country, but installations were made so rapidly that by 1988 more than 900 million cubic meters of gas were burned, often instead of oil or coal. Denmark has achieved energy self-sufficiency in oil. It still imports coal to fuel some power plants, but others have converted to burning gas.

The Danes realize that fossil fuels will not last forever, and to prepare for the long term the government has promoted both conservation and renewable energy. Conservation began in earnest during the energy crisis of the 1970s. Improvements in home insulation and government sponsored replacement programs for inefficient energy use proved successful. Between 1970 and 1988, there was a 0.9% annual decline in energy use even as the economy continued to grow. In recent years, increasing car ownership has undercut these savings somewhat, but fuel economy has improved because the annual road tax is low for energy efficient cars while it punishes gas guzzlers. As a result, there are not many sports utility vehicles. Denmark has also pioneered the use of windmills to produce electricity, and is one of the world's leaders in this area. Danish companies have sold about half of the world's installed windmill production, measured in kilowatt hours.

Deregulation has also been on the Danish energy agenda. The electricity market was partially liberalized on January 1, 2003, allowing free competition between providers. Yet, to prepare for the eventual decline of oil and gas reserves, consumers must buy a fixed percentage of their electricity from non-polluting alternative sources. As a result, the traveler sees ever more large white windmills along the Danish coastline.

Employment

In the workplace Danes are less hierarchical than the British or many other Europeans. Workers expect to have open and informal dialogue with management, and on most projects teamwork plays an important part. Getting angry is a poor tactic with Danish workers, who appreciate informality and a good sense of humor. The vast majority of Danish workers are union members, which accounts not only for their high wages but also for a good work-safety record.

However, because wages and taxes are high, black-market work does occur (because it costs less), particularly in plumbing, electrical work, and other home repairs. Unemployment, a problem in the 1980s, declined and briefly all but disappeared after 2002. During the world financial crisis that began in 2008, however, many jobs disappeared. By 2012 there were 2.6 million Danes working, but another 230,000 were unemployed. A good many of those without work were new university graduates who have not lost a job but are looking for one for the first time. One must increase this figure considerably, however, because roughly 235,000 people have been declared unemployable and given early retirement or invalid pensions. When one adds to these the 950,000 people receiving regular old age pensions (in a population of 5.4 million), the need to keep everyone else hard at work becomes obvious.

Taxes

To pay for its welfare state, Denmark has the highest overall tax rate in the world. More than half of all personal income is taken in tax, and a 25% VAT (called MOMS) is imposed on all goods and services, including books, food, and clothing. Even if they have clever accountants, most Danes pay half their income back to the state. Some items are singled out for additional taxes, such as automobiles (more than 120%), tobacco, and distilled alcohol. In recent years, this taxation has produced a budget surplus in good years but drops quickly into a deficit whenever unemployment rises above about 5%. Whoever is in power, be it the socialists or the conservatives, searches continually for ways to cut expenditures, primarily in order to meet the rising costs of health care and pensions.

The Welfare State

While Denmark appears to outsiders to be a model welfare state, with security from the cradle to the grave, it is struggling to define how much welfare it can actually afford. About 60% of the employed are engaged in community, social, and personal services or in public administration and defense, while the remaining 40% engage in agriculture, manufacturing, construction, trade, banking, business services, and insurance. Danish politics of the past 25 years has chiefly been concerned with how to cut back the number in services and administration, while increasing the productivity of the rest of the work force.

Agreeing on where to cut is difficult, because all political parties share a commitment to free hospital care, free education, and free care for the aged. Unemployment benefits are among the most generous in Europe, yet it is politically unpopular to cut back in these areas, even among many businessmen, who at times lay-off workers for short periods to save payroll expenses. They can do so without a bad conscience, because the short-term unemployed receive almost as much in benefits as they would in wages if working.

Lacking other targets, the government often threatens public employees with redundancy, and has sought to save money by cutting training programs. However, the chief effect of any financial crisis is that people who retire are not replaced. When services are reduced, volunteer work is not usually substituted, as this solution is extremely unpopular in a highly unionized country. Public sector workers are almost all in unions, whose contracts and regulations protect them from firing or replacement by less expensive foreign labor.

In current debates, Danes remain loyal to the idea of a welfare state that secures health, education, and fundamental services for all citizens. However, they have also become willing to accept new private hospitals, which serve those with money who dislike being on a waiting list. This privatization of the delivery of services has perhaps saved some money, and further savings are anticipated through computerization. Nevertheless, the focus is not on whether the welfare state is a worthwhile ideal, but rather on how to retain it. Few Danes seem to want a health system like the one in the United States, for example. The current hope is that through better management and more efficient organization a high level can be maintained.

Copenhagen's harbor.

Politics

Denmark is a constitutional monarchy, in some respects like Great Britain. There is a well-loved and accomplished queen, Margrethe, and a royal family that performs ceremonial functions, while leaving all practical affairs of state to the *Folketing*, or parliament. Unlike the American or the British system, however, the *Folketing* consists of one chamber, which has 179 deputies. There once was a higher chamber, somewhat like the House of Lords or the French Senate, but it was abolished by an amendment to the constitution in 1953. All citizens over 18 have the right to vote, and over 80% of them usually do. As in Britain, members of the *Folketing* elect the Prime Minister, who serves only as long as a majority supports him, and loss of support leads to an immediate election.

However, here the resemblance ends. In Denmark, any party that commands just 2% of the popular vote wins seats in the *Folketing*. This system produces many political parties, several of which are always close to extinction as their support hovers around 2%. In such a system, it is unlikely that any party by itself will ever have a majority, and coalitions are necessary both to form a government and to pass particular pieces of legislation.

Because there are many parties, in theory virtually every group has a small say in government. Indeed, governments may be minority coalitions made up of three parties who constantly must look for additional support. The result of this system is to focus influence at the center of the political spectrum. Extreme parties of the right or left have little chance to exercise power. In contrast, centrist parties have a disproportionate influence, since they are usually needed to form coalitions and to pass legislation. The price of this kind of democracy is that decisive action can prove difficult, and most legislation is arrived at by compromise. When combined with an extensive bureaucracy, such a system ensures that Denmark usually is slow to alter its institutions.

And yet significant change does occur. Until 2006, Danish local government consisted of a large number of cities and towns organized into ten provinces. The Danish central government decided, however, that there were too many units of administration and it restructured the system into just five regions. At the same time, it merged many smaller communities to form units of at least 20,000 people, but preferably 30,000. Not only did it impose this new political order from the top, but some formerly regional matters, such as spending on museums and cultural events, disappeared from the regional budgets. This dramatic reorganization process, none of which was submitted to a national referendum, shows the power of the central state in Denmark. No elections were held to see if voters approved of being reassigned to new capitals of new provinces. The restructuring is intended to make government more efficient, though it will be further from the grassroots. This much is certain: many mayors and other local officials have lost their jobs, large investments are needed to accomplish the reorganization, and many citizens now will have to travel further to get to their local authorities.

In the last decade, Danish politics has moved somewhat to the right. But compared to most other western countries, the spectrum of political parties still is considerably to the left. Danish Conservatives model themselves not on Margaret Thatcher's Tories but Tony Blair's Labor Party. They accept many features of the welfare state already in place and they oppose nuclear energy. Parties do not always act as one might expect.

In the 1980s, to improve the state's economy the Conservatives required a hefty involuntary "loan" from all citizens that fell most heavily on the wealthy, and they reduced the amount of interest that home-owners could deduct from their income taxes. They could not be accused of holding supply-side economic theories. Such role reversals were not limited to the Conservatives. In the 1990s, the Social Democrats promised to eliminate long hospital waiting lists but they refused to engage in deficit spending to do so. With conservatives raising taxes in the 1980s and social democrats running up budget surpluses in the 1990s, Danish political ideologies are obviously idiosyncratic. But to complete the confusion for an outsider, in 2001 a conservative coalition came into power, ostensibly to promote the free market and business.

Yet, in practice it clamped down hard on immigration, making it difficult to recruit talent from abroad, while its educational policies at first seemed calculated to drive some of the best Danish talent away.

Do not be confused by such things, however, because a secret of Danish politics is that the parties agree on a great deal. Overall, regardless of their ideology, almost all Danish politicians embrace free education, free medical care, and old-age pensions for all. Even those on the far left accept the constitutional monarchy, and no one clamors to stop paying taxes to the Lutheran church. Furthermore, virtually all Danish politicians accept same-sex marriage, free abortion, and equal rights for women. Indeed, the social consensus extends to a large number of rules and regulations that a foreigner only gradually notices. The national consensus also includes a widespread rejection of the death penalty, of nuclear power, and particularly of nuclear weapons. In short, politicians in Denmark often must work hard to create the illusion that important differences exist between them.

Foreign Affairs

A thousand years ago Denmark controlled half of England, and even today there is a rich heritage of common words in the two languages. The country was long a powerful force in Europe, controlling at various times present-day Norway, southern Sweden, parts of northern Germany, and other areas fringing the Baltic Sea. During the Renaissance Copenhagen was at the geographical center of a large state at a time when Germany and Italy were divided into many small independent entities.

Since the Napoleonic Wars, however, Denmark has not been an important military power, especially since the unification of Germany under Bismarck. This was achieved partly at Danish expense, as they lost the

Gay couples can marry in Denmark.

Schleswig-Holstein provinces (roughly speaking, the area north of Kiel) in the war of 1864. Some of the lost territory was later restored, based on a plebiscite after World War I. Iceland was part of Denmark until it broke away during the Second World War, leaving only Greenland and the Faroe Islands. Both of these have considerable autonomy in domestic affairs, but their foreign relations are in Danish hands.

In the 1920s and 1930s Denmark steered a neutral course, but nevertheless Germany occupied it during World War II. In the post-war period the country was a reluctant founding member of NATO, having first sought a Nordic Alliance as an alternative. Although it remains a member of NATO, Denmark has never allowed atomic weapons on its soil and has consistently sought détente. Given its geographical position between East and West, as well as its commitment to a welfare state, Denmark was uncomfortable with the polarization of the Cold War, and many citizens would have preferred a more neutral posture, especially during the American war in Vietnam. Not surprisingly, Danish government support for the policy of détente increased during the transitional years when Mikhail Gorbachef was the Russian leader. Danes were among the first to support independence for Lithuania, Estonia, and Latvia, and they were delighted to see the Berlin Wall fall.

Indeed, the opening up of eastern European economies places Denmark in an excellent economic and political position. Scandinavian political systems are regarded as models by many former communist countries, which are anxious to embrace capitalism while retaining extensive social services. In addition, Denmark's superior agricultural techniques and its mastery of high technology make it an attractive trading partner, not least because it is a small nation that by definition is non-threatening. Indeed, Poland has allowed some Danish farmers to purchase land in order to look over their shoulders and learn advanced agricultural techniques.

Denmark has always been cautious in approaching integration within the EU. In 2000 the nation voted against joining the new EU currency, for example, and still shows no signs of changing its mind about that. (Given the excessive deficit spending in the Euro currency nations, even in Germany, this may prove a wise decision.) Denmark did not join the EU at its inception, but first applied for membership in the European Community in the early 1960s. It was admitted in 1973. Even in 1972, when membership was submitted to a national referendum, the campaign was acrimonious. 90% of the voters turned out, and a surprising 36% of them were against joining. This minority sentiment has weakened, but has by no means died out. In the European Parliament some of Denmark's 16 seats long have been held by The People's Front Against the European Union. After twenty years of membership, in a 1992 referendum a slim majority rejected the Maastricht Treaty, fearing that the closer union it proposed would compromise national sovereignty. Even those who supported the European Union worried that the Danish language and heritage could be over-run by the cultures of larger countries. A subsequent compromise worked out in the Edinburgh Agreement proved satisfactory to the Danish voters, however, and smoothed the way for greater economic cooperation.

While these events put Denmark in a weak position inside the EU, more recently it has been able to play a key role. When Denmark was president of EU in the fall of 2002, it was responsible for the final negotiations that admitted ten new nations. Despite wrangling over agricultural subsidies and other matters, the difficult negotiations succeeded, and all ten candidate countries were admitted at the summit meeting in Copenhagen. Denmark was proud to play this role in definitively changing the map of Europe and ending the political divisions of the Cold War.

A key element in Danish foreign policy is advocacy for human rights. For example, Denmark consistently condemned the Franco dictatorship in Spain, and it campaigned to investigate human rights violations in Greece during the period of military dictatorship between 1967 and 1974. Likewise, Danish law long forbid trade with South Africa, until it elected a Black majority government.

Denmark has been a strong supporter of the United Nations since its inception, and has often provided troops for international peace-keeping, notably in Bosnia, the Congo, Cyprus, and the Gaza Strip. Most recently, however, the Danish government decided to work outside the framework of the UN, as it sent troops to keep peace in Iraq after the American-led invasion of 2003. This decision is not particularly popular inside Denmark.

Finally, Denmark has long been one of the most generous nations when it comes to foreign aid, almost all of it administered through the Danish International Development Agency (DANIDA). Indeed, independent organizations have often rated Denmark the world's best both in terms of the quantity and the quality of aid, after weighting comparisons for country size. Since Denmark had only tiny island colonies on the west coast of Africa and in the Caribbean, its assistance to the Third World is not shaped by a colonial heritage. Development efforts have focused on Africa and Asia, particularly on a few countries, notably Thailand, Bangladesh, Nepal, Kenya, and Tanzania.

Unfortunately, in recent years the level of aid was cut slightly. It remains to be seen whether declining aid donations and participation in the occupation of Iraq will be short-term anomalies or signs of a shift to the right in foreign policy. One clue to the future is the violent Moslem response in 2005 to cartoons, which appeared in the Danish newspaper Jyllands-Posten, that satirized the prophet Mohammed. All portraits of the Prophet are anathema to Moslems, and they provoked large demonstrations, including several that became violent and led to the burning of Danish embassies. Much of the nation was shocked and angry. Cartoons appear in every western

Moslems exercising western-style free speech to protest publication of cartoons they found insulting.

society, daily mocking leaders, and they are an accepted part of the democratic tradition of free speech. Danes had a hard time understanding how their long tradition of welcoming refugees and their continual service as international peacekeepers could be rewarded with such hatred and violence. As an intensely secular society, most were suprised by a crisis based on religion, and they were disappointed that many traditional allies, notably Britain, were at best lukewarm in their support.

Practical Advice for Visitors

Get Registered

The first thing anyone who plans to live in Denmark must do is obtain a "personal number" and the identity card which goes with it. You need this before you can do almost anything. Without a personal number, you cannot use the medical system, borrow a library book, open a bank account, rent an apartment, or start a job. You have a legal responsibility to register immediately on arrival, so do not travel around first. The card is national, but the registration is local, and must take place in the town where you plan to live. Registration is free, but note that it does make you a part of the Danish system of taxation.

Tourists who fall in love with Denmark should also note that there is no automatic right to register and live in the country, and that in almost all cases one must apply for permission to do so <u>before arrival</u>.

Once you are registered and have a personal number, you still need a valid passport from your own country. If your passport is near expiration, you can arrange for a new one with your embassy in Copenhagen, but do so at least one month in advance of the expiration date.

Travel inside Denmark

Transportation systems in Denmark are extremely well developed, so that in many instances you will have several ways to reach a destination. Automobiles are often not the cheapest way to go, particularly when traveling between the major cities. The state railway (DSB) operates trains every half-hour or even less from Copenhagen to Odense, and every hour to Århus. These main line trains are new and comfortable, and they run faster than a car can legally cover the same distance. The trains are coordinated with bus lines, ensuring that smaller destinations are linked into one national system. Within local areas, cycling is often the fastest alternative, and with separate bicycle lanes on most major streets, this option is safe and particularly attractive in the summer months. Indeed, some people explore the whole country on bikes, which can be taken on all ferryboats and most trains, usually at little or no cost.

For those who insist on driving, be forewarned that car rentals may cost more than in much of the rest of Europe, and gasoline prices are high. On the other hand, most distances are short, and the roads generally are in fine condition. Exceeding the speed limit is costly, however, and motorists must pay fines if hidden cameras show that they have been speeding. So drive with care, and keep an eye out for cyclists, remembering that they have as much right to be on the road as cars do. When turning either right or left, remember that you must give way to cyclists who are continuing straight on. If you are in any doubt about traffic regulations, ask for further information at a tourist office or car rental agency. One last important note: driving while under the influence of alcohol is considered a serious offence, and it is punished more severely in Denmark than in much of Europe. Danes risk getting a large fine if caught out on the highway after taking more

Front page of The Copenhagen Post.

than one or at most two drinks. If stopped by the police, you do not have the right to refuse a breath test, and it is exceedingly unlikely that you can escape the penalties. On the bright side, such tight regulation makes the Danish roads safe.

Working in Denmark

Do not expect to find a part-time job while in Denmark. Tourist and student visas do not permit outsiders to work, though restrictions on EU citizens are far less stringent than on others. In any case, most jobs require knowledge of Danish, so it is not wise to expect to find a job soon after arrival. If you know you want to work in the country, consult the Danish Embassy in your home country about the regulations, and begin to search for work before you arrive. The following websites may be useful.

- The Ministry of Research urges highly skilled white-collar workers to consider moving to Denmark. http://www.workindenmark.dk/
- The Danish Immigration Service provides information at http://www.udlst.dk/english/default.htm
- The Ministry of Foreign Affairs encourages investment in Denmark. http://www.investindk.dk/default.asp?artikelID=9664

Finding Accommodation

For most short-term residents finding a place to stay is a difficult task. Danish universities try to help visiting students, but their resources are limited. Since housing is a perpetual problem even for Danes, there is often little real help available through official channels. If you are offered a room, think twice before turning it down. Because demand is greater than supply, few rental apartments are advertised in the newspapers, and most information travels by word of mouth. One option for students is to sub-let one room in an apartment, which will not only solve the housing problem but will put you in daily touch with some Danish people.

What to bring? What to buy?

Prices are higher in Denmark than in many other EU countries. The Danish value-added tax of 25% applies to everything, while additional taxes are slapped on luxury goods such as whiskey and airline tickets. (You may be able to get some of these taxes refunded when leaving the country, so get a Tax Free Shopping Guide and learn the rules.) Medicine, until recently fully subsidized but no longer, costs more than in Sweden and in some cases is double the Italian price. Bring supplies of medication that you need, small personal items such as perfume and aftershave, the legal limit of cigarettes if you are a smoker, and most of the clothing you need. Except for mink coats, stylish Danish clothes are likely to cost as much or more than in your home country. Furthermore, fine gradations in size generally are not available for items such as shoes or men's shirts. Danes are well dressed but casual, which is appropriate considering how many bicycle to work.

Students take note: textbooks are expensive in Denmark. A paperback textbook may well cost 1 kroner per page. Books published in English-speaking countries, which are used in many science courses, cost about double their English or American price. If possible, obtain reading lists in advance and acquire texts before you leave home.

The Danish Climate

By American or Mediterranean standards, it is never really hot in Denmark. The mean temperature in July is only 17.1 C. Temperatures over 25 are rare, and a day over 30 is considered extraordinary. Given this mild summer, little wonder that almost no Danish buildings have air conditioning. By the same token, by Russian or Canadian standards, it is never really cold in Denmark either. The temperature is not often below freezing for days on end, and snow seldom covers the ground for much of the winter. When selecting a wardrobe, also remember that most Danish buildings are well insulated, centrally heated, and quite comfortable in winter. Visitors should prepare for damp, cool weather, like that along the coast of Scotland or in northern Japan. Umbrellas and waterproof shoes will be useful.

Average Temperatures in Denmark												
	Jan	Feb	Mar	Apr	May	Jun	Jul	Aug	Sep	Oct	Nov	Dec
°C	– 0.4	– 0.4	1.3	5.8	11.1	15.4	17.1	16.6	13.3	8.8	4.1	1.3
°F	31.3	31	34	42	52	60	63	62	56	48	39	34

Holidays in Denmark

Holidays are not universal. As you might expect, all stores and banks are closed on Christmas, the day after Christmas, and New Year's Day. But there are some distinctively Danish holidays that you should also note.

April 16, the Queen's birthday, is also a day of national celebration, though not all institutions close down for it.

June 5 is Constitution Day *(Grundlovsdag)* and all institutions close down.

June 23, St. Hans Evening, is an important moment in Danish life, when crowds mark the arrival of midsummer by lighting large bonfires at dusk and singing patriotic songs.

There are also four important spring holidays whose dates vary. These holidays are religious in origin: Easter, Store

Bededag, Ascension Day, Whitsunday. Note that Easter is really a five day weekend, as it includes the Thursday and Friday before and the Monday afterwards.

Learning Danish

What about the Danish language? The bibliography here lists several works that can help English speakers learn the language, but it is advisable to look for texts in your mother tongue and start from there. It is a very good idea to attend a Danish course as well, preferably before arriving, or as soon after arrival as possible. If the Danish institution you are affiliated with offers no instruction, in larger communities there are late afternoon and evening classes offered at a modest cost. Be prepared for a mixed group of students, including political refugees from outside Europe, with a wide variety of native languages. As a result, the only common language in class usually will be Danish, which is therefore the language of instruction. The emphasis will probably be on speaking the language, with grammar being explained at more advanced stages as it becomes necessary. Intermediate and advanced classes generally also give some attention to explaining Danish culture and institutions, since one of the goals of instruction is to integrate refugees and immigrants into the society.

There are many textbooks and recordings to help you learn Danish, with new ones appearing every year. Find one that moves directly from your first language to Danish. If your mother tongue is Japanese, German, or French, do not use an English textbook. The same goes for dictionaries, and fortunately Danish publishers have made bilingual dictionaries available for all the major languages.

Libraries and Books

If you are moving to Denmark for an extended period, it still may not be necessary to bring many books. Most libraries also have a representative selection of foreign magazines and periodicals. Note that the larger libraries have many books in English and some in German, including novels, so it should not be necessary to bring leisure reading with you. Scholarly holdings are spotty, depending upon the field, but usually are good for materials published since 1960. Newly installed computer systems speed the search for books inside the country. Cutbacks have hurt some libraries, however, so recent acquisitions may be incomplete in the humanities, though better in social sciences and science.

The more Danish you learn, the more resources you will be able to use. For those just trying to get started, here are a few reliable books about Denmark that have appeared in English. For more titles, check local bookstores and libraries after you arrive.

- Bredsdorff, Thomas et al., 100 Danish Poems: From the Medieval Period to the Present Day. Seattle: University of Washington Press, 2011 & Copenhagen: Museum Tusculanum Press, 2011.
- Jansen, F. J. Billeskov, and P. M. Mitchell, Anthology of Danish Literature. Carbondale: University of Southern Illinois Press, 1971.
- Jespersen, Knud J. V., A History of Denmark. London: Palgrave Macmillan, 2004. [from the Reformation to the present.]
- Levine, Ellen, Darkness over Denmark: The Danish Resistance and the Rescue of the Jews. Holiday House, 2000 [for children aged 9-12.]
- Pundik, Herbert, In Denmark it Could Not Happen: The Flight of the Jews to Sweden in 1943. London: Gefen Publishing House, 1998.
- Stewart, Jon, Kierkegaard and His Contemporaries: The Culture of Golden Age Denmark. Holland: Walter de Gruyter, 2003.
- Thomas, Alastair H., and Stewart P. Oakley, Historical Dictionary of Denmark. Lanham, MD: Scarecrow Press, 1998.
- Thomas, F. Richard, Americans in Denmark. Carbondale: Southern Illinois University Press, 1990.

Danish National Newspapers

Danes buy newspapers per capita twice as often as the French, the Italians, or the Spanish, and despite being a small nation there is a wide selection. You may be amazed that you can begin to understand the newspapers fairly soon after arrival, with the use of a dictionary. Almost every Danish town has a newspaper, and it is a good source of information about housing, sales, and public events.

B.T. and *Ekstra Bladet* are similar to the *London Daily Mirror* or *New York Daily News*. For new arrivals, they may not be easy to read, because the language used often contains puns, slang, and currently popular expressions.

Politiken, is a lively left-liberal newspaper that maintains a healthy critical attitude toward the government, offers a reasonable coverage of Denmark and does its best to cover the rest of the world as well.

Information, is more to the left on most issues than *Politiken*. It accepts few advertisements, and firmly signals it does not want to cover sports, the stock market, or business, but it has interesting and acerbic views on politics, social issues and culture.

Berlingske Tidende is somewhat to the right of *Politiken*, and would probably seem to be a moderate or slightly left-leaning were it available in other countries. For those in or near Copenhagen, it has the largest Sunday listings for jobs, houses, apartments, and the like.

Jyllands-Posten in recent years has broadened itself from being a provincial newspaper in Jutland to being a national paper. Of late it has been rather shrill in its coverage of Danish culture, however, and on occasion seeks to provoke (as with its infamous cartoons of Mohammed), but it has good coverage of business and international politics.

Last words

Little more than a generation ago, a visit to Denmark almost automatically became a total cultural immersion. This was a good thing. It forced the long-term visitor to confront the language and the culture, and to grow and learn from the experience. It is harder to escape from your home country today. In the age of the Internet and cheap long distance telephone calls, keeping in touch with events back home can be so easy and regular that it can pose a problem. Surely, the goal of living abroad is to go as deeply as possible into a new cultural world. Yet this may be difficult when major foreign newspapers are generally available at the larger newsstands and in railway stations, and when family and friends are only an e-mail away. Ideally, try to limit communication with friends and family to a restricted period each day, and do not waste the opportunity to know another country by reading newspapers from back home on the Internet.

Denmark's University Webpages

- Copenhagen Business School: www.cbs.dk
- Copenhagen University: www.ku.dk
- DTU – Denmark's Technical University: www.dtu.dk
- IT University of Copenhagen: www.itu.dk
- Roskilde University: www.ruc.dk
- The Royal Veterinary and Agricultural University: www.kvl.dk
- SDU – University of Southern Denmark: www.sdu.dk
- Aalborg University: www.aac.dk
- Aarhus University: www.au.dk

Calling Denmark from abroad

The European Union, Eastern Europe, and China	00 45
Much of South America and Africa	00 45
Sweden and Nigeria	009 45
USA, Canada, Japan, Hong Kong, South Korea, Singapore	001 45
Mexico	00 98
Australia	00 11
Russia	8 10 45

For other nations, see a telephone book